DL 126
Grades 5-8

Personal Projects

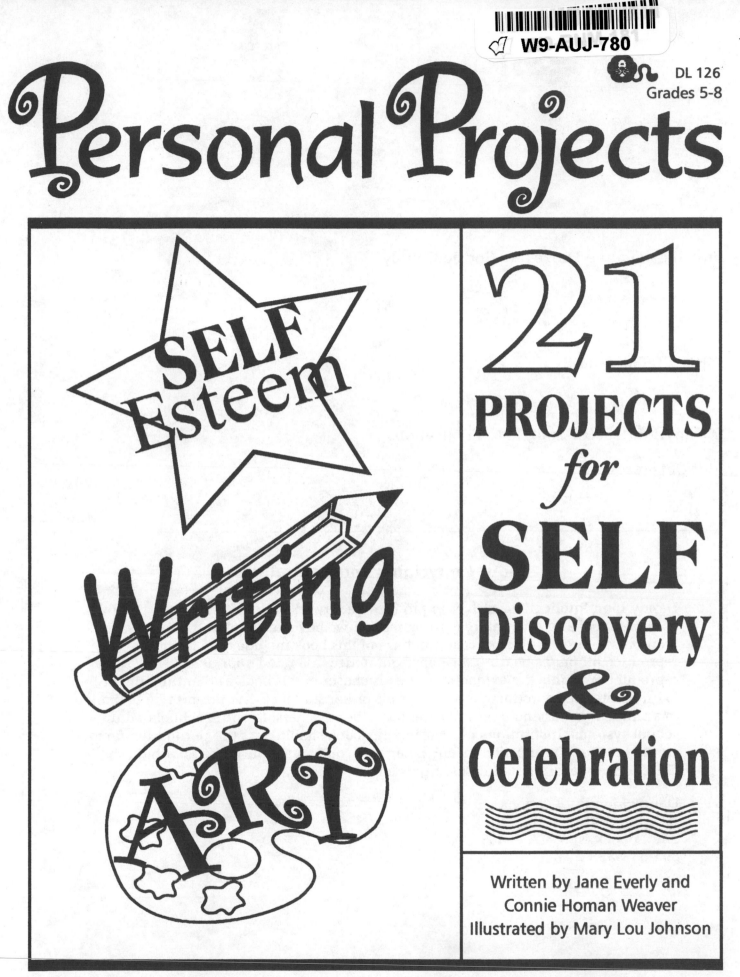

SELF Esteem

Writing

ART

21 PROJECTS *for* SELF Discovery & Celebration

Written by Jane Everly and
Connie Homan Weaver
Illustrated by Mary Lou Johnson

Edited by Dianne Draze and Sonsie Conroy

ISBN 1-883055-34-2

About Copyrights and Reproduction

Table of Contents

To our families: Greg, Samantha, Laurie, and Matthew,
for all your love and patience.

The purpose of *Personal Projects* is to address students' affective needs. Affective skills deal with an ongoing attention to one's internal states – the ability to access one's own feelings, discriminate among these feelings, and draw on the feelings to guide one's behavior. Students must develop these skills in order to

- move beyond extrinsic motivation to intrinsic motivation
- manage their emotions
- experience personal growth
- accept and appreciate themselves
- relate positively to other people

Personal Projects addresses these affective skills by using a unique combination of art and creative writing that encompasses introspection, creativity, and communication. The use of art adds a powerful dimension of validity to student writing. It allows for deeper, more meaningful expressions of feelings, of personal value, and individuality.

The activities in this book will:

- deepen self awareness and appreciation
- boost self-esteem
- promote exploration and expression of feelings
- validate individuality and identity
- encourage creativity
- enhance personal growth
- prompt healthy attitudes toward self and others
- develop the ability to express oneself in writing

Using this Book

Each lesson in this book includes educational **objectives**, a list of **materials** that will be needed for the lesson, step-by-step **procedures** for conducting the lesson, and a brief overview of what type of **evaluation** will take place after the projects have been completed. Most lessons involve a **writing activity** and an **art project.**

Lessons, especially those with more involved art projects, may require several class sessions to complete. Allow enough time for students to do the self-reflection that is required prior to beginning the writing and art components and also enough time to successfully complete the projects. The end result should be much more than just a showy art project. It should provide an opportunity to learn something about oneself.

Because of the personal explorations involved by some of the activities, it is extremely important to create a safe, accepting classroom climate, one in which all contributions are welcomed, not ridiculed. Teachers should explain to students that information written and discussed as a part of these activities will be held in the strictest confidence. Students should always have a choice about having their work displayed, read aloud, or published.

The lessons in this book are divided into four sections. These four sections are Symbolism of Self, Color Your World, The Nature of Life, and Reflections.

- **Symbolism of Self** activities help students develop self-knowledge and self-expression by using various symbols.
- **Color Your World** activities help students explore feelings and relationships through the use of color.
- **Nature of Life** activities give students the opportunity to examine their feelings through comparisons with various things in nature.
- The activities in the **Reflections** section help students build character through activities that explore emotions, memories and relationships.

Materials and Supplies

Keep these general supplies on hand for students to use with the various activities. Some of these materials may trigger more creative thinking than mere pencil and paper.

ART Supplies

- old newspapers and magazines
- cardboard
- empty toilet paper or paper towel tubes (cardboard)
- scissors and X-acto knives
- glue, glue sticks, rubber cement, hot glue
- construction paper
- posterboard in a variety of colors
- mat board
- sketchbook paper
- crayons and markers
- watercolor and acrylic paint
- egg cartons
- fabric remnants
- string
- paintbrushes
- masking tape
- sponges
- spray bottles
- paint containers
- graph paper
- modeling clay
- paper plates
- Styrofoam cups
- glitter, sequins, other sparkly items
- wrapping paper
- straws
- wallpaper wheat paste (powder)
- old wallpaper sample books
- a "grab" bag or box of scrap materials such as buttons, ribbon scraps, and other "junk" materials

Writing Tools

- thesaurus
- dictionary
- notebook, portfolio, journal, or sketchbook
- computer, word processor, or typewriter
- lots of clean paper
- trash can
- pencils, pens, erasers

Self Collage

Overview

Students will explore and express their individuality and uniqueness in a collage.

Objectives

- The student will design and create a collage that represents his or her uniqueness.
- The student will develop an acceptance and appreciation of self.

Materials Needed

✓ magazines and newspapers
✓ half sheets of posterboard (a variety of colors)
✓ scissors and glue sticks
✓ copies of page 8

Procedure

❝ Discussion

1. Using the following questions as a guide, discuss individuality and uniqueness with your students:
   - How do you define individuality?
   - In what ways do you express your individuality?
   - What makes you unique?
   - Why do you value being unique and different from others?

✍ Writing Activity

2. Distribute copies of page 8. Ask students to fill in this chart.

✂ Art Activity

3. Distribute magazines and newspapers. Ask students to find and cut out pictures, words, or phrases that in some way symbolize their uniqueness. These cut-outs can be favorite things, personality traits, meaningful qualities, special hobbies, or descriptions.

4. Distribute posterboard pieces. Ask students to arrange and glue their cut-outs on their posterboard in a way that represents their uniqueness. Before gluing materials, have them think about an attractive layout. For example will the elements all be in a straight line or grouped according to a common theme? Will the pictures be on one side and the words on another, or will the words and pictures form a design such as a spiral, stripes, or heart?

Evaluation

- Design and arrangement of items on the collage
- How well the collage represents the student's uniqueness

Extension

Self Poems - Create self poems out of words and phrases cut out of magazines.

WHAT  MAKES ME UNIQUE?

Adjectives that describe me	My favorite things are	My most positive qualities are
My special interests or hobbies are	Things that make me happy are	I feel important when
When I grow up, I want to	My best subjects in school are	I am proud of
I love	I have strong opinions about	My favorite colors are

HEAD LINES

Overview

Students will explore their feelings by writing poems about themselves that are showcased in the silhouettes of their heads.

Objectives

- The student will develop an acceptance and appreciation of self.
- The student will develop a combination art and writing product that depicts his or her inner thoughts.

Materials

✓ large sheets of black and white construction paper or posterboard
✓ grab bag supplies
✓ chalk
✓ copies of page 11
✓ glue

Procedure

✄ Art Activity

1. Divide students into pairs. Have student A use the overhead or slide projector as a spotlight to shine on black paper taped to the wall. Student B should sit in the light beam between the projector and the paper so that the silhouette of his or her head or head and shoulders clearly shows against the black paper. Student A is to use chalk to draw around Student B's shadow on the black paper. When this process is complete, place a new piece of black paper on the wall and have students reverse roles.

2. When the black silhouettes are drawn, have students carefully cut them out, dust off the chalk or turn the silhouettes over so the chalk does not show, and paste to them to a white sheet of paper serving as the background.

✍ Writing Activity

3. Distribute copies of page 11. Have students complete the statements to form a poem about their thoughts, dreams and feelings.

Once this poem is complete, have students creatively combine it with their silhouettes. They can use a light colored paint pen to write the poem in the silhouettes, either in parallel lines or in the shape of a spiral, or they can use different colored markers to write the poem on the white background around the head.

Students should feel free to visually emphasize their thoughts using other grab bag supplies such as glitter or sequins to elaborate on this basic design.

Evaluation

- Creativity and expressiveness presented in the writing project
- Creativity and insight demonstrated in the combined art/writing product

Extensions

Headache Silhouette - Using the same head silhouette, write about things that weight heavily on your mind, or " headaches."

Writing - Write a short essay on the topic of being headstrong, what it means, when it causes problems, and when it can be considered a positive characteristic.

Head Line Poem

Complete the following statements. Then use your answers to write a poem about the things going on in your head.

My mind is filled with

Concern for _____,

Ideas about _____

and _____,

Dreams of _____,

_____,

and _____,

Feelings of _____

and _____,

And hopes for _____.

Sample Poem

My mind is filled with
Concern for the sick and hungry,
Ideas about improving my grades and creating new music,
Dreams of nature's beauty, spending time with far away friends, and world peace,
Feelings of sadness when I think about the problems my best friend is having and
of joy when I am greeted by my new puppy,
And hopes for a future filled with friends and love.

Like-A Poem

A Personal Simile

Overview

Students will identify their individual personality characteristics and compare these characteristics to familiar objects.

Objectives

- The student will develop an acceptance and appreciation of self.
- The student will identify characteristics of his or her personality through the use of similes.
- The student will demonstrate creative writing skills.
- The student will show creative use of color and design through artistic enhancement of the simile poem.

Materials Needed

✓ copies of pages 14 - 15
✓ unlined white paper
✓ notebook paper
✓ markers, colored pencils, and crayons
✓ computer for word processing (if desired)
✓ pens and pencils

Procedure

66 Discussion

1. Involve students in a pre-writing brainstorming session in which they identify a variety of personality characteristics or traits. Some of these traits may include being shy, outgoing, cheerful, stubborn, assertive, or loyal (see appendix). Together make a long list. After the list is completed, ask each student to write down six of his or her individual personality traits for use in the simile poem.

Explain to students that the Like-A poem will help them to better understand their personal characteristics through the use of similes. Define a simile as a comparison of two things using the words "like" or "as." Give students the following examples (or examples from literature) and then ask them to verbally volunteer other examples of similes.

✓ *She sat as still as a stone.*
✓ *She bounced around the room like a rabbit.*
✓ *Like a swan, she gracefully floated down the stairs.*
✓ *Under his calm exterior he was as nervous as a caged wild animal.*
✓ *Her personality was as complex as a Mozart symphony.*

Writing Activity

2. Distribute copies of pages 14 and 15 and ask students to write the Like-A poem using this format, comparing their different personality traits to the items on the list and beginning each line with the words "Like a." Give an example or two from the sample poem on page 14 and explain to students that they should not write a comparison unless they also include an explanation of how they are like that object. An inappropriate response would be *"I am like a bird."* An appropriate response would be *"I am like a bird, always spreading my wings in different directions."*

The finished poems can be typed or written neatly on unlined paper and enhanced by the following art activity.

✂ Art Activity

3. Have students create a design or logo for their names using large, colorful lettering. This will serve as the title for their poems. This title should be placed above the poem. It may be cut out and pasted on, drawn, or painted. Have students create a matching border or design for the rest of the page.

Evaluation

- Characteristics that accurately describe the student
- Fluent use of similes
- Creative use of color and design to visually enhance the poem

Extensions

Family Members - Students can write Like-A poems about different members of their families. These can be framed and given as gifts.

Family Poems - A Like-A poem can also be written about a family as a whole. A family name can be used as the title and each of the lines should be a comparison of that family to different objects. For example:

The Hendersons
Like busy beavers at the dam,
    always working together and bustling about,
Like a supreme pizza,
    mixed with many unusual combinations.
Etc.

Amanda

Like a tree, standing tall and strong in the midst of a crowded forest.

Like a rabbit, always hopping around from one thing to the next.

Like the colors yellow and red, at times sunny and warm hearted, and at other times angry and grouchy.

Like bread, always loafing around.

Like a hair dryer, sometimes blowing hot and cold.

Like a pebble, lost in a sea of boulders.

Like a Chevrolet, built to last and attractive to look at.

And like a can of cola, sometimes effervescent, but occasionally I go flat.

14

Creating a *Like-A* Poem

1. Write your Like-A Poem on notebook paper, following the format listed below. Each response will be considered a line in the poem. Begin each line with the words "Like a/an... (name the object)" and explain why you are comparing your personality to that particular object.

2. The only line that is slightly different from the rest is the third one, in which you compare your personality to two colors. For this response, you are to write in this manner: "Like the colors ____ and ____, at times I am _____, and at other times I am _____," explaining how the colors show two different sides to your personality.

3. When you have finished, write or type your poem neatly on an unlined sheet of paper, leaving room for a large title. The title will be your name, written colorfully and creatively at the top of the page. Add an accompanying border or design around the rest of the page.

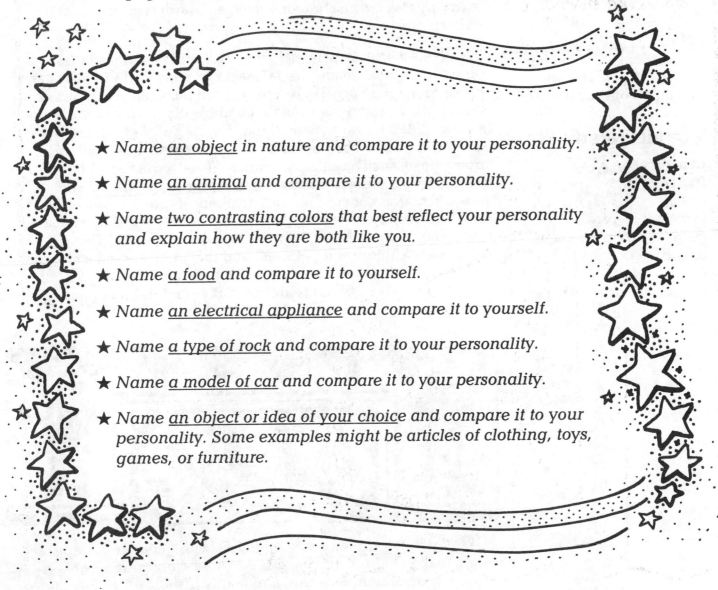

★ *Name <u>an object</u> in nature and compare it to your personality.*

★ *Name <u>an animal</u> and compare it to your personality.*

★ *Name <u>two contrasting colors</u> that best reflect your personality and explain how they are both like you.*

★ *Name <u>a food</u> and compare it to yourself.*

★ *Name <u>an electrical appliance</u> and compare it to yourself.*

★ *Name <u>a type of rock</u> and compare it to your personality.*

★ *Name <u>a model of car</u> and compare it to your personality.*

★ *Name <u>an object or idea of your choice</u> and compare it to your personality. Some examples might be articles of clothing, toys, games, or furniture.*

MASKING FEELINGS

Overview

In this activity, students will design, create, and decorate a mask that represents of their inner selves or feelings.

Objectives

- The student will develop an awareness of his or her inner feelings.
- The student will develop an acceptance and appreciation of self.

Materials Needed

✓ paper mâché materials (newspaper, wallpaper paste)
✓ copies of page 18
✓ crayons, colored pencils, or markers
✓ paint
✓ balloons (1 per student)

Multi-Cultural Connections

Masks have been used in many cultures for a variety of ceremonies and traditions. In **Japan**, Noh theater is a highly stylized form of drama that uses masks. Movements are slow and exaggerated. Actors use pantomime to improvise gestures and pacing appropriate to each mask. Experts describe a powerful transformation that occurs once the mask is donned, through which the actor becomes one with the mask. Perhaps this helps explain why some African and Native American tribes ascribe magical power to masked rituals or why masked celebrations, such as Mardi Gras can easily get out of control.

Native Americans believed in many spirits. To please these spirits, some tribes made special masks to wear during dances and ceremonies. These ceremonies were often performed to teach or remind people about their religion and history. Masks were made in many different ways, using the materials people found in their surroundings. The simplest mask was made from the head of a large animal, such as a deer or buffalo. The Iroquois and Northwest Coastal tribes carved wood into masks. Some tribes wove masks from grass or corn husks. Members of the Iroquois Falseface Society wore carved wooden masks when they appeared in healing ceremonies for ill or injured tribe members. These masks were painted and polished, and they represented a special dream in which a man had seen a spirit. In the Southwest, Zuni and Hopi tribal celebrations and holy days include Kachinas, spirits portrayed by masked members of the tribe.

West African tribes decorated masks with geometric shapes relating to their culture and ancestors. These cultural motifs often symbolized religion, proverbs, and family history.

Procedure

66 Discussion

1. Ask students to brainstorm and name as many different masks as they can, along with the reason a particular mask is used. Ideas may include surgical masks to protect people from germs, catcher's masks to protect athletes from injury, gas masks to filter the air, Halloween masks to conceal identities, snorkeling masks to facilitate underwater vision.

Discuss psychological "masks" such as putting on a good face for the world to see, camouflaging yourself to fit in, and masking your true feelings. Ask students to volunteer examples of times when they or others used a psychological "mask" to protect themselves. Discuss the fact that masks are also used to represent other things (people, animals, or intangible things) in celebrations and ceremonies. Discuss how masks could represent one's feelings or personality traits.

✂ Art Activity

2. Distribute copies of page 18. As a class or in small groups, generate a set of symbols and colors that represent different feelings and/or personality traits. Ask each student to use these symbols to design a mask that represents his or her inner self.

3. Distribute balloons. Tell students the balloons will be inflated and used as bases for creating three-dimensional paper mâché masks. Half of the balloon will be covered with paper mâché to form a mask. They may tape rolled newspaper or cardboard shapes on to the inflated balloon to form eyes, mouths, or other facial features.

After the bases of the masks are complete, have students apply two to four layers of paper mâché. Each layer should be smoothed and allowed to dry before adding the next layer. When all layers are completed and the paper mâché has dried, have students pop the balloon so that all that remains is the mask form. Students may wish to trim the edges with scissors.

4. Provide students with a variety of acrylic paint colors with which to decorate their masks. Students may wish to use spray paint for a base. Be aware that many spray paints are oil-based and acrylic paint will not adhere to oil-based paint.

Encourage students to attach objects onto their masks after the paint is dry. They may wish to add hair, whiskers or jewelry.

✍ Writing Activity

5. When masks are completed, ask students to write a paragraph that begins, "I am not always what I appear to be."

Evaluation

- How well the student's mask represents his or her selected feelings
- Creative use of color and design
- Depth expressed in creative writing

Extensions

Writing - Ask students to describe a time when they had to mask their feelings.

Drama - Use masks to create a classroom drama, pantomime, or skit.

MASK DESIGN

Draw and color your mask design in this box, then complete the statements that follow. Use the back of the paper if necessary.

The colors I used in designing my mask are _____

These colors represent _____

The symbols I used in my mask are _____

The overall shape of my mask signifies _____

My mask depicts my personality because _____

_____

Package and Advertise Yourself

Overview

Students will create products that represent their personalities and will advertise the products.

Objectives

- The student will identify his or her personality traits.
- The student will design, construct, and present creative packaging for a product that represents his or her personality.

Materials Needed

- ✓ writing paper
- ✓ containers (bag, bottle, box, or can)
- ✓ construction paper or other colorful paper
- ✓ markers, colored pencils, or crayons
- ✓ copies of pages 21 - 22
- ✓ cardboard or mat board, as needed

Procedure

66 Discussion

1. Initiate a class discussion about the uniqueness of people. Encourage students to focus on the following:
   - Everyone is unique. Each person has different characteristics that make him or her special.
   - Everyone has a talent for something. At times those talents are hidden deep inside, known only to that person, and not always recognizable to others.
   - Sometimes it is hard to identify our own talents.
   - It is important to maintain your individuality and not be easily influenced by peer pressures.

2. Ask each student to make a list of character traits and/or talents that make him or her special or unique.

3. Distribute copies of page 21. Ask students to look at the product list and find a product that best symbolizes them. Ask some of the following questions to activate their thought processes:
   - How do you see yourself as a grocery store product?
   - Are you canned, bagged, boxed or bottled? Why? For example, a canned person may be someone who is secure in a small space, perhaps they might be shy. A bottled person may have lots of laughter waiting to explode.
   - How are you like the actual product itself? What characteristics do you share with it? For example, a soft drink and a person could both be bubbly. A candy bar and a person could both be sweet.

Writing Activity

4. Distribute copies of the planning sheet on page 22. Have students complete the questions. After they have described their product and container, they should creatively write their personality characteristics in the form of a list that sounds like ingredients for their products. An example of personal ingredients for a candy bar might be:

energy	sweetness
laughter	caution
compassion	intellect
fun	ambition

Then students should create names for their products that include all or part of their own names. For example, a girl named Lex might name a candy bar "Comp**LEX**ity" and a boy named Jim might call his vitamin product "Vita-Jims."

Have students write slogans to advertise their products. These should be short phrases to get people's attention and succinctly state the main features of the product.

Finally students are to write jingles (short poems or songs) about their self-products. The jingles will be used in their commercials.

✂ Art Activity

5. Have each student design and create an original package that represents his or her product. They may bring an appropriate container from home to decorate. All labels and graphics on the container should be covered up with attractive and creative new labels. The following information should be included on each product package:

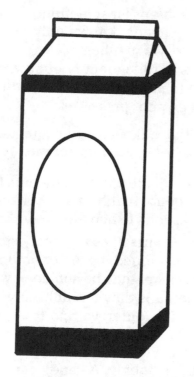

- the name of the product
- who made this product; for example Lex and Co.
- a list of personality ingredients
- a logo (a visual symbol of the product)
- the slogan
- any other details or illustrations that will enhance the product, such as a picture of the student

 Presentation

6. Have students create a commercial for their self-products. For this part of the project they are to make live or videotaped two-minute presentations that incorporate their slogans and jingles.

Evaluation

- The creativity and completeness of the product and commercial. Assign points for the following things for a total possible score of 100 points:
  - ➤ name selection
  - ➤ packaging design
  - ➤ ingredient listing
  - ➤ slogan
  - ➤ logo
  - ➤ commercial (including a jingle)

Extensions

Radio Advertisement - Have students create radio spots to advertise their products.

Magazine Advertisement - Have students create one-page magazine spreads to advertise their products.

Advertise Yourself
Project Guidelines

1. Select one of these products and advertise yourself as the product.

soft drink	*candy*	*can of vegetables or fruit*
cereal	*pasta*	*spaghetti sauce*
bread	*chips*	*crackers*
can of soup	*shampoo*	*detergent*
pretzels	*vitamins*	*toothpaste*
salad dressing	*band-aids*	*milk product*

2. Complete the product planning sheet. Include all of the following in the design of your self-product:

   Name - Create a name for your product that contains all or part of your name.

   Package - Use the type of package in which the product is normally packaged. Cover the original container with an attractive label that represents your personality. Choose your favorite colors and design a logo to go under the name of the product. Add other details to make the packaging more interesting and attractive.

   List of ingredients - Choose things that best represent you and your personality traits and talents. An example of the ingredients for someone's candy bar might be:

energy	*sweetness*
caution	*compassion*
fun	*ambition*
laughter	*intellect*

   Slogan - Create a memorable slogan for your product that will be used on the package and in your commercial.

3. Create your package.

4. In addition, create a **commercial** for your self-product. This will be a live or videotaped presentation that is two minutes in length. It should include a short jingle.

Advertise Yourself
Planning Sheet

1. The type of product I have chosen to represent me is _____

2. The type of container my product will be packaged in is _____

3. The name of my product is _____

4. Sketch of my product's logo

5. My product's ingredients are (should represent your personality) _____

_____

_____

_____

6. My product or company's slogan is _____

_____

7. My jingle (a short poem or song) is _____

_____

_____

_____

22

A Slice of Life

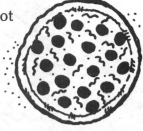

Overview

Using a pizza metaphor, students will create free-verse poems and pizzas that represents their personalities.

Objectives

- The student will demonstrate self-knowledge.
- The student will demonstrate the ability to draw comparisons between his or her own traits and the elements of a pizza.
- The student will write a poem analyzing his or her personal characteristics.
- The student will design a pizza and pizza box that represents himself or herself.

Materials Needed

✓ cardboard or mat board
✓ pens and pencils
✓ black felt-tipped pen
✓ an empty pizza box for each student (12" minimum size)
✓ round aluminum pizza pans to use as patterns
✓ construction paper in a variety of colors
✓ sequins, buttons, glitter, and fabric
✓ scissors
✓ copies of pages 25 - 26

Procedure

66 Discussion

1. Ask students to think about all the different features of a pizza and list these on the chalkboard. They should include, but not be limited to the following:
   - crust: thin, pan, hand-tossed, flaky, stuffed
   - tomato sauce: chunky, spicy, zesty, mild, tangy
   - chees
     e: melted, mozzarella, Parmesan, Cheddar, burned, spilling over
   - toppings: pepperoni, anchovies, mushrooms, olives

   Discuss each of these attributes and how they can metaphorically relate to a person's life or personality. Some examples are:
   - A crust is the foundation for a pizza, and a person's family or religion might serve as the foundation or "crust" of his or her life.
   - Pizza sauce might be spicy or mild, and a person might be considered spicy if he is angry or quick-tempered.
   - Cheese can be burned on top, and we can get "burned" by friends we trust. Cheese can be bubbly, and we can happily bubble over in our enthusiasm.

   Ask students what kind of pizza best represents their personalities. Are they a single topping? Combination? Supreme? Do they have a lot of ingredients or just a few?

2. Read through the sample poem on page 25. Instruct students to examine each part of the pizza and compare it to aspects of their lives such as personality traits, hobbies, talents, or disposition. Ask them to write their own comparisons in the form of a free verse poem.

   Distribute copies of page 26. Have students write the final drafts of their pizza poems on this sheet. They will eventually paste this to the inside of the pizza box lid in the following art activity.

✂ **Art Activity**

3. Distribute pizza boxes. Explain to students that they are going to create a pizza to go in this box. First have them trace around a round pizza pan on cardboard or mat board. Have them cut out this circle, which will serve as the crust of the pizza. You may be able to get these round cardboard shapes from pizza restaurants or at a hobby store in the cake decorating department.

Have students layer the pizza with sauce and cheese cut from construction paper or other scrap materials.

Then have students add the toppings that were mentioned in their poems. Use hot glue to attach three-dimensional objects. Creativity should be encouraged, but students should be certain that their pizza actually resembles a pizza.

4. Have students make a small legends or keys that show which personality traits are represented by each pizza topping. Have them glue these, along with their poems, to the inside of the pizza box lids, so that when you open the boxes, the charts and poems will become visible.

5. Have students decorate the outside of the pizza boxes by creating attractive labels with the names of their pizzas on them. The name of the pizza should use a part or all of the student's name. Be sure to have students cover all existing company names on the box with the labels they designed.

Evaluation

- Use of metaphors or similes to describe personality traits
- Depth of personal insight reflected in poetry
- Creative use of materials to make the pizza
- Creativity of pizza box and name of the pizza company

Extensions

Party and Awards - Have a pizza party at which students design and award certificates for the most creative pizza, most insightful poem and any other categories they feel are appropriate.

Delivery System - Pizzas are often delivered. Ask students to devise a delivery system for positive messages in the class.

A Slice of My Life

Sample Poem

Study the following sample pizza poem. Then write your own pizza poem that describes your personality.

A Slice of My Life

I am a supreme pizza, a blend of many things.

I am the crust, firm and unyielding in my beliefs.

I am the sauce, varied in depth, but still consistent overall

I am the stretchy cheeses, many different flavors melted into one.

I am the peppers, small and innocent on the outside, energetic and dangerous within.

I am the onions, unnoticed until it's too late to stop.

I am the squishy mushrooms, soft and sensitive.

I am the extra cheese on top, hiding it all inside.

I am the pizza. I AM ME!

By Philip P.

A Slice of My Life

SHADES of SELF *Color Poetry á la Andy Warhol*

Overview

Students will compare different feelings or moods to colors and use these comparisons to write a poem.

Objectives

- The student will develop an awareness of different feelings.
- The student will demonstrate self-knowledge by completing the writing activity.
- The student will demonstrate knowledge of the Andy Warhol's color technique by completing the art activity.

Materials Needed

✓ writing paper
✓ pens and pencils
✓ watercolor paints
✓ three or four photocopies (black and white) of each student's school photograph
✓ color wheels
✓ crayons
✓ glue sticks
✓ construction paper
✓ copies of page 29

Background Information

Andy Warhol was a modern artist who led the "pop art" movement that began in the 1960's. He painted anything from soup cans to pop bottles and often painted these common household items in enormous proportions. He was further recognized for his silk-screened repetitive paintings of famous people such as Marilyn Monroe and Elvis Presley. His "Triple Elvis" painting showed three of the same pictures of Elvis silk-screened on an aluminum colored background canvas. At times, Warhol used three to four duplicate pictures of people and painted them with unusual colors to highlight faces, hair, background, and clothing.

Procedure

66 Discussion

1. Ask students to generate a list of feelings. Record these on the board. Compare these feelings to colors. For example, orange might be excitement, green might be tranquility, and blue might be sadness.

   Ask students to think of their own moods or feelings and record these on a sheet of paper and then choose colors to represent these feelings.

✍️ Writing Activity

2. Distribute copies of page 29. Ask students to use the sample and format to create a poem that uses three colors to symbolize three very different aspects of their moods or feelings. Students should have access to a color wheel or large box of crayons to get color ideas.

✂️ Art Activity

3. Bring in examples of Andy Warhol's art, so students understand the different styles they will be trying to duplicate.

4. Ask students to bring to class a recent school photograph or other clear head shot of themselves. Photocopy each of these at least three times on a copier using a light print setting. Enlarge photographs if necessary.

Distribute photocopies to students. Ask them to lightly paint (using water colors) each of their photocopies using the Andy Warhol technique.

Each copy should be painted with only the three colors used in the poem, and each copy should be painted differently. For example, one face might be green with yellow hair and red clothes, another face might be yellow with red hair and green clothes, and the third face might be red with green hair and yellow clothes.

5. Cut out the three painted photocopies and mount them on construction paper or mat board.

Display the art with the color poem or glue them on facing pages of a sketchbook journal.

Evaluation

- Depth of self-knowledge demonstrated in the writing activity
- Awareness of feelings demonstrated in the writing activity
- Use of color to represent different feelings or moods

Extensions

Picasso Poems - Write poems using Picasso's art as a model.

Research - Have students research and report on the work of Andy Warhol or Picasso.

COLOR POETRY *á la Andy Warhol*

Select three colors that best represent your moods or feelings. Using the outline below, write a three-color poem that tells how your feelings or moods are like these colors. The poem should consist of nine lines. The first line of each stanza should begin with the words "At times I am ____ (a color). The next two lines should creatively compare this color to specific moods or feelings.

Sample Poem

At times I am red,
Angry like a giant volcano ready to erupt,
And like a blazing fire, lashing out at everyone.

At times I am yellow,
Filled with incredible joy and happiness,
Like a sunflower, reaching out to everyone.

At times I am green,
Jealously yearning for what I don't possess,
Envying all the beautiful creatures in this world.

Write your poem here.

At times I am _____,

_____,

_____.

At times I am _____,

_____,

_____.

At times I am _____,

_____,

_____.

Presentation of Colors

Overview

Students will create shields to represent their personal identities.

Objectives

- The student will develop an acceptance and appreciation of self.
- The student will express his or her individuality through heraldic symbolism.

Materials

- ✓ copies of pages 32 - 34
- ✓ crayons or colored pencils
- ✓ sheets of cardboard for shield backing
- ✓ red, yellow, black, white, green, blue, and purple posterboard or construction paper
- ✓ glue (if using posterboard)
- ✓ glue sticks (if using construction paper)
- ✓ scissors
- ✓ X-acto knives or box cutters (mat knives)

Multicultural Connections

Native American warriors made and used circular shields for protection. These shields carried the warrior's identity via a collection of symbols, each having a distinct meaning in and of itself or in combination with other symbols.

A man made his shield carefully and decorated it with designs from dreams or designs that represented his tribe or family clan. Special feathers and small bags of amulets were tied onto the shield for good luck. The shield was displayed in a special place in the home and was usually buried with the man when he died. Plains warriors carried shields into battle to give them additional spiritual powers. The drawings on the shield were chosen to provide special powers: bears meant strength, turtles implied long life, and birds represented swiftness. Because warriors tried to capture shields in battle, a man carrying a shield was more likely to be attacked.

Tribal cultures of Africa used shields in much the same way as Native Americans. Their shield designs, rich in cultural heritage, depicted faces or geometric patterns on elongated, rather than round, shields.

Procedure

66 Discussion

1. Define identity as "the distinguishing character or personality of an individual; individuality." Initiate a class discussion through questions such as:
   - Discounting physical appearance, what makes your identity different from others?
   - Is your identity more than your personality? Why or why not?
   - Do you want your identity to be positive or negative? Why?
   - What pictures or shapes can you use to represent your identity and differentiate it from others' identities?
   - What colors symbolize you?

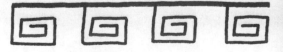

2. Distribute the heraldry sheet (page 32). Discuss each component of a knight's identity and how he was distinguished from all other knights even when he was covered by a suit of armor.

✂ Art Activity

3. After discussing the three main components of shield designs, ask students to express their identities through the creation of shields. Have them use the rules of heraldry (page 32) and the outline on page 33 to do this. After their designs are complete and you (role playing the herald) have approved them, ask students to create a large shield using the following steps:

a. Using the overhead or opaque projector, project the shield outline on page 33 onto a large piece of cardboard so that the distance across the top of the projected shield is about 18 inches. Using a pencil, trace around the projected outline on the cardboard. Then cut the cardboard shield out using an X-acto knife or mat knife. This first cardboard shield may be used as a pattern for the rest of the class to trace so they can cut out their own shields. (You can also prepare these cardboard shield backs the students prior to class if you do not wish students to use the knives).

b. After students have cardboard backs for their shields, have them recreate and cut out the components of their shield designs using colored posterboard or construction paper. The posterboard cut-outs should be pasted on the cardboard backing so that the cardboard is completely covered and does not show.

✍ Writing Activity

4. When these shields are complete, ask students to write down how and why their shield shows their identities (page 34). These may be taped on the back of the shields so that students retain their privacy when their shields are displayed.

5. Then have students incorporate the ideas that they have outlined on page 34 into well-organized paragraphs that explain how their shields represent their identities.

Evaluation

- Use of color to depict personal identities
- Use of the rules of heraldry in the design of the shield
- Clarity of written explanation of shield elements

Extensions

Writing - Ask students to think about shields as a means of protection and make a list of shields in their lives (parents, homes, clothing, peer groups, etc.). Then ask each student to select one shield and write a story about when he or she felt protected by that shield.

Cultural Connections - Create a self shield based on designs from another culture, such as Native American or African.

Heraldry

Heraldry is a very old visual language originally used to identify knights. Men in armor looked alike, so each knight chose a symbol and color(s) that distinguished him from all the others. Knights displayed this form of identification on their shields. Men called heralds were given the responsibility of keeping records of these designs. Shield designs had up to three basic components.

1. Parting of the Field

The field is the surface of the shield. Shields of more than one background color are divided by lines. These lines do not have to be straight; they may be wavy or zig-zaggy. These lines simply divide the background into sections of different colors.

2. Charges

The symbols and figures used to decorate shields are called charges. These charges are usually divided into two categories: Ordinaries (usually geometric designs such as stripes, borders, crosses or chevrons) and other devices such as animals, suns, or objects.

3. Tinctures

In heraldry, tincture means color. There are two categories of heraldic tinctures:

Metals – The two metals are gold (yellow) and silver (white).
Colors – The traditional heraldic colors are red, blue, green, purple, and black.

The rule of tincture states that no metal should be placed alongside another metal and no color should be placed adjacent to another color. The light tints of the metals are more easily seen when placed against the darker colors, which was the original reason the rule was made – easy visibility in battle.

The symbolism of the traditional tinctures is:

yellow / gold - honor and loyalty
red - courage
black - grief
purple - high rank passion, or suffering

white / silver - faith and purity
blue - piety and resolution
green - youth and vitality

Heraldry

Use heraldic tinctures, divisions, and charges to create your own coat of arms on the shield outline below. You may choose to use the traditional symbolism in your shield design or you may identify your own symbolism for these colors.

After your
design is com-
plete, enlarge this
design on posterboard
or cardboard to create a large shield.

My Identity Shield

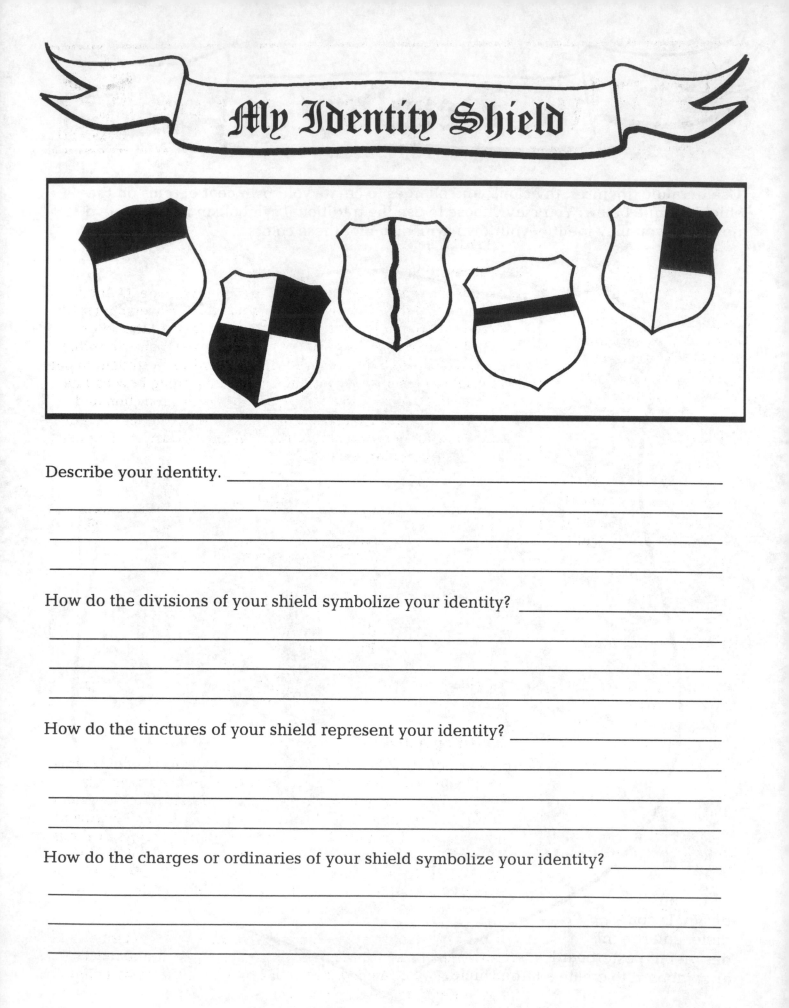

Describe your identity. _____
_____
_____
_____

How do the divisions of your shield symbolize your identity? _____
_____
_____
_____

How do the tinctures of your shield represent your identity? _____
_____
_____
_____

How do the charges or ordinaries of your shield symbolize your identity? _____
_____
_____
_____

Blue Jean's Letter

Overview

Students will identify feelings that are expressed in a letter written by an imaginary schoolmate. They will then empathize with the emotions expressed by this student and write a response.

Objectives

- The student will explore his or her feelings about teasing and harassment.
- The student will develop a tolerance for individual differences.
- The student will demonstrate empathy.

Materials Needed

✓ copies of page 37
✓ pencils or pens
✓ markers, crayons, colored pencils, or paint
✓ unlined white paper
✓ rubber cement or hot glue
✓ denim material or blue paper
✓ scissors
✓ grab bag of decorative items

Procedure

66 Discussion

1. Ask the students to carefully read the letter on page 37 and to imagine that they were once students in Jean Haversham's 4th grade classroom. After students have silently read the letter, initiate a class discussion about the feelings and emotions that must have been felt by Jean at the time. Ask each student to put himself or herself in the author's place, imagining how bad he or she would feel if forced to experience Jean's rejection and verbal abuse. Each student should take a few minutes to meditate on his or her own contributions, if any, toward student harassment in similar situations.

✍ Writing Activity

2. Have students write a letter responding to Jean. They may write to the fictional Jean or to a real person whom they have mistreated in the past (fictional names may be used to protect identities). In this letter, they should apologize for past offenses and tell what they intend to do to improve matters in future dealings with this person or with others who may be victims of harassment. If the letter is directed to a real someone, students are not required to send it, but should place it (as a reminder) in the blue jean pocket described below.

If a student feels that he cannot respond to Jean's letter because he, himself, is frequently a victim of peer harassment, then it might be a good idea to allow that student to write his own letter from Jean's point of view.

✂ Art Activity

3. Have students make large blue jean pockets for their letters. These can be made from blue paper with drawn-on stitching or from blue material. Pockets should be glued on an attractive background with rubber cement or hot glue. Students should then decorate their pockets using materials from the grab bag. These decorations may include logos, bandannas, buttons or sequins.

Have students put the letters to Jean in the decorated jeans pockets.

Evaluation

- Demonstration of empathy in the response letter
- Letter that is well-organized and grammatically correct
- Creative embellishment of the pocket

Extension

Behavior Codes - Ask the students to create their own personal behavior codes to deal with harassment of peers. Conduct a classroom meeting in which each student contributes his or her best ideas for a class code. Compile the ten best responses into one document for the classroom. Allow a few students from the class to design a decorative poster with the code written on it. Post this in a prominent place in the room and refer to it often.

Dear Class,

I am writing this letter from my new home in Fairfax, Virginia. You probably won't remember me, but I felt the need to write this letter anyway. I was in Mrs. Shipley's fourth grade classroom with all of you. My seat was in the very back of the room on the row near the window. I had to sit there because no one wanted me to be anywhere near them in the room.

I remember one day I made the mistake of putting my books on one of the desks in the front of the room. Several of you, I don't know who, knocked over the desk and all of my books fell to the floor. Somebody grabbed my book bag and dumped my lunch out too. When my drink bottle began to roll, somebody kicked it until it smashed up against the wall, leaving a big red stain all over the floor and wall. When Mrs. Shipley came back to the room, she asked who did it and no one spoke up. You all just looked at me and pointed. She told me to clean up the mess, and I did. All of you were laughing the whole time. When I went back to my seat, one of you put your foot in the chair and wouldn't let me sit down.

It was like that every day, and sometimes it was worse. Someone once took a pair of scissors and cut a piece of my hair; and on several different days, people took my lunch or lunch money. You all called me names like "Ugly" or "Stinky" and made fun of my clothes. It hurt a lot and nobody seemed to care very much.

What you didn't know is that my father died the summer before, and my mother had to work three different jobs to make ends meet for us. There were some days that my mother sacrificed and gave me her food so I would have lunch. At one time during the school year, we were evicted from our house, and we had to live in our car for a month. There was no bathtub or deodorant for us to use. Finally we moved into a shelter, and for a little while we had a roof over our heads and enough food.

Things have changed for me now. My Aunt Mary came and got us, and we live with her and Uncle Jim in their house here in Virginia. My mother only has to work one job. I have friends, and people treat me like I'm a real person. The year after I left your class, I took a bottle of pills, and I almost lost my life. Thank goodness for the kind people in this community. I have found myself again. Those of you in that fourth grade class need to know this so you won't go on treating people so horribly. I am, sincerely yours, a new person (a happy one) now.

Yours truly,

Jean Havisham

OPPOSING VIEWPOINTS

Overview

Students will think about opposing sides of an issue, will write about both viewpoints, and will create an art project that shows positive and negative.

Objectives

- The student will demonstrate the ability to debate both sides of an issue.
- The student will demonstrate persuasive writing skills.
- The student will create a work of art showing positive and negative space.

Materials Needed

✓ writing paper
✓ pens or pencils
✓ construction paper
✓ scissors
✓ glue sticks or rubber cement
✓ copies of pages 40 - 41

Procedure

66 Discussion

Discuss why it is important to be able to see different points of view. What are the advantages of being able to see things from another person's perspective?

> Two writing assignments accompany this activity. Although they are different from each other, both can easily be used with the same subjects and should be displayed with the art project for this lesson.

✍ Writing Activity 1

One way to prepare and motivate students for this activity is to conduct a "silent debate" about a topic. Pair up students and let each pair decide who will take the positive or negative side of the silent debate. Have the positive person write about the positive side of the subject or issue and the other person write about the negative side of the issue. Each side will be given one minute to write their ideas. Then students should trade papers and respond in writing to what their partners have written. Then they switch roles; the positive person now writing about the negative side, and the negative person writing about the positive side. Then they respond to what their partners have written. There should be no talking during this "debate."

Distribute copies of page 40. Ask each student to select one of the topics listed and think about the positive and negative sides of the topic. Ask each person to write two paragraphs: one reflecting positive aspects of the topic and one representing the negative side of the topic.

✍ Writing Activity 2

Distribute copies of page 41. Familiarize students with the format of a diamante poem. Discuss the example given on the handout. Ask students to create a diamante using a topic from the list or one they select.

✂ Art Activity

Step One - Ask each student to design a symbol that represents his or her writing topic. After sketching several options on scratch paper, students should select their favorite design to use for the art project. Some examples might be snowflakes or spirals for winter, a flag or cluster of stars for freedom, or a row of paper cut-out people (all the same) for popularity.

Step Two - Have students draw their symbol the size of a piece of construction paper and cut it out to use as a pattern. Then have students cut their pattern in half, preferably in such a way that the two halves are symmetrical.

Step Three - Have students to select two contrasting colors (one light and one dark) of construction paper for this project. Have them trace around one half of their pattern (from step two) on one color and the other half of their pattern on the other color. Have them cut these out and set them aside.

Step Four - Distribute one additional sheet of each of the selected colors. Have students cut the light sheet in half and paste one of the halves on the dark sheet of paper as shown below. This will be the background.

Step Five - Have students place their design cutouts (from the third step) together so that the two halves create a whole. Glue the design on the background created in the fourth step so that the light half of the design is on the dark half of the background and vice versa.

Evaluation

- Art project demonstrating the use of positive and negative space and the use of contrasting colors
- Selection of a symbol to represent the chosen topic
- Creative writing reflecting two viewpoints, perspectives, or opposite ideas

Extension

Points of View Writing - Have students tell about a real incident in their lives from three different points of view; one from a personal point of view and two others from the perspectives of other people.

POSITIVE **NEGATIVE**

Select one of the topics listed below. Think about the issue from a positive and a negative viewpoint. Write one paragraph reflecting a positive stance on the subject and another paragraph representing the negative side of the subject.

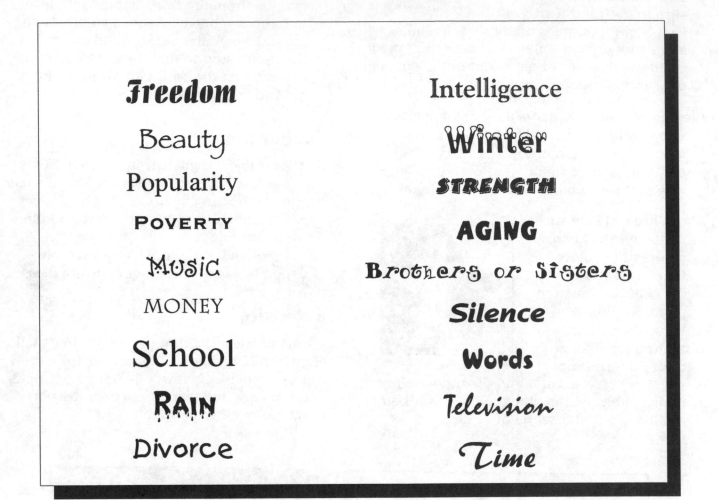

Freedom

Beauty

Popularity

POVERTY

Music

MONEY

School

Rain

Divorce

Intelligence

Winter

STRENGTH

AGING

Brothers or Sisters

Silence

Words

Television

Time

OPPOSING VIEWPOINTS

A diamante is a diamond-shaped poem with seven lines. The first word and the last word are opposites. The poem is a comparison of these two opposing subjects.

line 1 - first subject (a noun)

line 2 - two adjectives describing the first subject

line 3 - three ing-words related to the first subject

line 4 - four nouns or phrases, two related to the first subject and two related to the second subject

line 5 - three ing-words related to the second subject

line 6 - two adjectives describing the second subject

line 7 - the second topic that is opposite of the first subject

Sample Diamante

Silence
Profound, Tranquil
Settling, Waiting, Drifting
Quiet, Stillness, Motion, Clamor
Aggravating, Disturbing, Pounding
Shrill, Harsh
Noise

Select one of the following topics or a topic of your own choosing and create a diamante about the topic and its opposite. Write your poem and illustrate it.

freedom
hope
happiness
morning
darkness
kindness

beauty
winter
cooperation
truth
love
divorce

Just Singin' the Blues

Overview

Students will identify annoyances or irritations in their lives and create blues-style songs about these problems.

Objectives

- The student will identify sources of stress commonly occurring in his or her life.
- The student will write a blues song about the stress in his or her life.
- The student will design a sculpture that represents this major stress factor.

Materials Needed

✓ writing paper
✓ pens or pencils
✓ copies of pages 44 - 46
✓ hot glue gun and glue sticks
✓ X-acto knives
✓ scissors
✓ paints, watercolors, and markers
✓ small blocks of wood about ½ to 1 inch high
✓ a box full of interesting supplies for the sculptures: mat board, glitter, sequins, dowel rods, toothpicks, pipe cleaners, fabric and wallpaper remnants, aluminum foil, Styrofoam plates and cups, ribbon, string, popsicle sticks, buttons, dry pasta and Mardi gras beads

Background Information

In the 1800's, black slaves working in the cotton fields in the south often made up songs while they worked. Someone would begin the song and eventually most of the people in the field would respond with new verses. These  songs were first called "field hollers." The work was long and hard, and the music helped people to forget about families and homes left far behind. The term "blues" means feeling sad or depressed, and the music is often repetitive and soulful. W.C. Handy is often referred to as the "father of the blues," because he was the first person to ever publish a blues song in 1912.

Procedure

66 Discussion

1. Listen to some blues music so students gain an understanding of this type of music before beginning the lesson.

2. Distribute copies of page 44. Ask students to list grievances, problems or stresses that make them "sing the blues" in their everyday lives. Have them list as many things as possible in each of the categories listed on the handout.

Writing Activity

3. Distribute copies of the sample song on page 46. Have students chant the refrain as you sing or chant the verses. This will give them the flavor of the "blues" rhythm. Ask students to select one of the listed problems or annoyances and write blues songs about how it makes them feel sad, frustrated or forlorn. Have students use the song format found on page 45. The sample blues song found on page 46 uses a common refrain pattern (dah DAH dah dah dah) that students may wish to use in their songs.

4. When students have completed their songs, they should present them to the class as dramatically as possible. They may use rhythm instruments and other class members to enhance their presentations. Between the verses, they may ask the class to sing the refrain.

✂ Art Activity

5. Ask students to think about and sketch several symbols that could represent the topics or sentiments depicted in their blues songs. In the case of the sample song, some suggested symbols might be dirty tennis shoes, blue jeans, caps, or toys. Ask each student to select the best symbol(s) for a three dimensional representation and hot glue the symbol to a wood base that has been previously painted. Any materials may be used to add to the basic design. For instance, someone might choose to represent money. Their basic symbol might be a large cardboard dollar sign. This symbol would then be embellished with play money, words from printed material, or other decorations. Once finished, each student should create a name plate for the sculpture. The sculpture title should be written or typed neatly on name plates.

Evaluation

- Completion of a blues song expressing a problem or frustration in life
- Completion of a three-dimensional representation of the subject of the song

Extensions

Research - Have students research famous blues musicians and the blues music movement.

Other Music Styles - Repeat the lesson using a different form of music (rap, country, or jazz).

Writing - Ask students to write stories about times in their lives when they were sad or blue.

Solutions - Have students write (in a positive context) about what they could do to alleviate, solve or lessen the problem they have identified.

Brainstorming the Blues

List all of the things that make you feel "blue" (sad, frustrated, lonely, down-in-the-dumps) for each of the following categories.

School

HOME

FAMILY AND FRIENDS

SPORTS

Social Events

Hobbies

Other Things

Just Singin' the Blues

Use the bottom of this piece of paper to begin writing a blues song about one of the problems you listed on the Brainstorming the Blues sheet. Use the following format to write your "tale of woe."

♫ Songs should consist of five to six verses of 3 lines each.

♫ The first and second lines of each verse should be the same length.

♫ The third line of each verse should be as long as line 1 and 2 combined.

♫ The second and third lines of each verse should rhyme.

♫ Insert a "refrain" or rhythmic pattern as indicated on the sample song; (something like dah DAH dah dah dah)

♫ The final verse should be different rhythmically from the rest. It should sum up all the frustrations in the song and end in "yeah" or "oh yeah!"

_____

_____

_____

_____

_____

_____

_____

_____

Continue on the back of this paper or on another piece of paper.

The Little Brothers Blues

Sample Song

1. *I was sittin' in my room (dah DAH dah dah dah)*
   Just the other day (dah DAH dah dah dah)
   Just mindin' my own business in a very happy way (dah DAH dah dah dah)

2. *I was talkin' on the phone (dah DAH dah dah dah)*
   To my best friend Flo (dah DAH dah dah dah)
   We were planning for the weekend, lots of shopping and a show (dah DAH dah dah dah)

3. *When all of a sudden (dah DAH dah dah dah)*
   I heard a very loud noise (dah DAH dah dah dah)
   Someone pounding and banging. It had to be...the boys! (dah DAH dah dah dah)

4. *They were my little brothers (dah DAH dah dah dah)*
   John Paul and Stephen Ray (dah DAH dah dah dah)
   Always annoying and disturbing me each and every day. (dah DAH dah dah dah)

5. *They run into my room (dah DAH dah dah dah)*
   And mess up all my stuff (dah DAH dah dah dah)
   They torture my poor dog until my mother yells "ENOUGH!" (dah DAH dah dah dah)

6. *I love them very much (dah DAH dah dah dah)*
   But sometimes they make me wail (dah DAH dah dah dah)
   They make me mad and angry and I wish they were for sale
   Oh, I wish they were for sale!

7. *I've got the door-bangin', phone-droppin', ear-splittin', head-hurting, make me scream*
   and yell, dog-torturing blues. Yeah!

Note the following components of the sample song and be sure to include them in your original song.

- Name the setting
- Tell what you are doing
- Introduce the problem
- Explain why it's a problem
- More information about the problem
- Bring it to a close, repeat the last line
- Change rhythm and end it–yeah!

46

TREE-mendous Metaphors

Overview

Students will identify with a tree or plant and use it as a metaphor to explore their inner selves.

Objectives

- The student will develop an awareness of his or her feelings and an understanding of self.
- The student will create a leaf-theme art project to complement their writing.
- The student will write metaphors to describe him or herself.

Materials Needed

- ✓ crayons, colored pencils, or paint
- ✓ fresh leaves of varying shapes and sizes
- ✓ unlined white paper
- ✓ colored construction paper for mounting

Procedure

66 Discussion

1. Ask the students to verbally list all the attributes of trees they can think of. List these on butcher paper, chalkboard or with an overhead projector. Be sure to include the following characteristics and feature:

- outer bark that protects the tree
- branches, and branch patterns
- types of roots
- types of leaves or needles
- leaf colors
- needs good soil, water, and sunlight to grow
- some grow in the forest, some grow alone
- weather affects them — bending in the wind and storms causes them to lose branches
- provides shelter to animals and other plants
- creates oxygen
- provides shade
- continually growing

Discuss the attributes and how they can also relate metaphorically to people's personalities. For example, you might tell students that trees have an outer covering of bark to protect their inner core. Ask them, "How do you protect your 'inner core,' and what aspects of your personality are like tree bark?"

Tell students that trees need light, water, and good soil to grow. Ask them, "What do you need to grow? And what nurtures your 'roots'?"

✍ Writing Activity

2. Explain that a metaphor is a comparison between two unrelated nouns. It is a direct comparison that states "___ is ___." It does not use words "like" or "as."

Ask students to select a tree that is most like their personality and/or represents who they are. Have each student compose a metaphor comparing his or her personality to this tree. Tell students to describe where this tree is located and what it looks like. Have them use the list of tree attributes generated earlier in the lesson to incorporate details about how their personalities or inner selves are like these trees.

You may wish to share an example of your own with your students. An example of the tree metaphor may turn out something like the following:

"I am a mighty oak, standing tall in the midst of a crowded forest. Although you can't always see me because of all the other trees, I stand up strong and tall for what I believe in. My tough outer bark of optimism and skepticism protects me from the world's criticism. My branches of learning reach ever outward toward the light of my future, while my roots ever deepen in the fertile soil of friends and family. Although the storms in life often remove parts of me, I steadily flourish, replacing the dead wood and broken branches of mistakes and failure with the new green growth of lessons learned. My towering limbs of love shield my younger brothers from the hot sun of injustice as they play in my shade."

---

3. Have students pair up to share their rough drafts, get feedback and suggestions from their partners, and then write or type their final copy very neatly on a clean unlined sheet of paper. This will be decorated in the next step.

✂ Art Activity

4. **Texture Rubbing** - Collect leaves of various shapes and sizes. Invite students to create a texture rubbing background or outline for their tree metaphor using the collected leaves and  crayons. To create texture rubbings, place a pattern of leaves underneath a sheet of paper. Using the SIDE (not the point) of a crayon, gently rub the front of the paper until the leaf patterns appear.

Have students mount their writing and their art work on colored paper that compliments the colors in the leaf design.

5. **Leaf Printing** - An alternative to the leaf rubbings is to do leaf printing around the border or on the matting. To do this, lightly paint the most textured side of a leaf with acrylic paint. Turn it over and press the painted side on the paper. The result is a print of the leaf's texture.

These make excellent and meaningful fall decorations for the hallway or classroom. Because of the personal nature of these metaphors, some students may not want to display their products. Remember to respect their wishes.

Evaluation

- The use of metaphors to describe personal traits and characteristics
- The use of color and design to enhance the written poem

Extensions

Other Metaphors - This process of creating a personal metaphor may be used with objects other than trees. Flowers work well for spring writing, and students always have an interest in animals and cars. Weather also may prove to be a revealing topic of comparison. You may also wish to choose objects related to a particular field of study such as sea animals when studying oceanography.

It's a Natural Thing

Overview

Students will choose an emotion and use similes to create a poem that compares the emotion to things in nature.

Objectives

- The student will demonstrate understanding of an emotion by comparing it to things in nature.
- The student will organize his or her thoughts in a poem.
- The student will design and create a border or background with a nature theme.

Materials Needed

✓ white drawing paper
✓ watercolors and brushes
✓ straws and paint (optional)
✓ black felt-tipped pens
✓ copies of pages 51

Procedure

❝ **Discussion**

1. Define the term simile as the comparison of two things using the words "like" or "as." Ask students to generate examples of similes. Example: *dances like an elephant, loud as a police siren, soft as new fallen snow, sings like a bagpipe in the hands of an amateur, old as a dinosaur.*

✍ **Writing Activity**

2. Distribute copies of page 51. Examine the sample and ask the class to generate several options for the last three lines of the sample poem about love.

3. Have students choose an emotion and create their own simile poems using suggested format. Do not allow students to use any of the ideas from the sample.

✂ **Art Activity**

4. Ask students to select one of the following art activities:

   a. Use watercolors to paint a scene from nature that represents the message of the poem.

   b. Paint an abstract watercolor background on white paper.

   c. Pour a blob of ink or paint on a white sheet of drawing paper. Using a straw, blow the wet ink or paint around the paper in different directions. Look for shapes in this painting that represent the selected theme.

5. After the paintings have dried, have students write their poems with a black felt-tipped pen so the poems are superimposed over the paintings.

Evaluation

- The use of similes to compare feelings to real things in nature
- Organization of similes to form a poem
- Use of creativity in the visual presentation of the art project

Extensions

Man-made Comparison - Have students compare emotions to common man-made objects.

Writing - Have students select a feeling from the list in the appendix. Then have them write paragraphs describing and giving examples of the chosen emotion.

It's a Natural Thing

1. Study this format for a simile poem and read the sample that follows. As a group, write the last stanza of this poem.

Title:	Use the selected theme as the title of your poem.
Line 1:	Use a simile to compare your theme to something in nature.
Lines 2-3:	Give two reasons why your theme is like this natural thing.
Line 4:	Use a second simile to compare your theme to a second natural item.
Lines 5-6:	Give two reasons why your theme is like this second natural item.
Line 7:	Use a third simile to compare your theme to a third natural occurrence.
Line 8-9:	Give two reasons why your theme is like this third natural occurrence.

❤ ❤ ❤ ❤ ❤ ❤ ❤ ❤ ❤ ❤ ❤ ❤ ❤ ❤ ❤ ❤ ❤ ❤

Love

Love is like a river,
Rushing happily along with never a care,
Blindly crashing into boulders along its path.

Love is like a flower,
Blooming brightly in the golden sun,
Its roots planted firmly in fertile soil.

_____

_____

_____

2. Select one of these feelings.

hope	*love*	*happiness*	*sorrow*
truth	*anger*	*peace*	*hate*
serenity	*loneliness*	*joy*	*despair*

3. Write a simile poem about your selected feeling.

Mapping Life's Journey

Overview

Students will create a map whose land forms, roads, and cities represent their life experiences.

Objectives

- The student will use metaphorical thinking to equate life experiences with typical geographical features.
- The student will design and create a unique map whose land forms, roads, cities, and bodies of water represent stages or milestones in his or her life.
- The student will write about his or her life experiences using metaphors to describe the experiences.

Materials Needed

- ✓ pencils/pens
- ✓ writing paper
- ✓ butcher paper
- ✓ crayons, watercolors, markers
- ✓ copies of page 54

Procedure

66 Discussion

1. Initiate a discussion about various life experiences. Ask students to visualize life in terms of a journey. Ask them these questions to get them thinking in that direction:
   - What is your destination? Do you have one?
   - Have you mapped out your trip or are you just driving where the road takes you?
   - What "escape routes" have you taken to avoid dealing with a difficult situation?
   - What are your "rest stops?"
   - Are you in the slow lane, the passing lane, or missing the right exits on life's highway?
   - Are you more like a large city, a small farming community, or a national park? Why?
   - How are hardships in your life like crossing oceans or scaling mountains?
   - What new frontiers have you explored? What ones do you hope to explore?
   - Do you ever get lost and have to ask for directions? What is your "compass?" From whom or what do you get your direction?

2. Distribute copies of page 54. Ask students to study the list of things they might find on a map, then metaphorically equate each of the geographical features to life experiences they have had.

✍️ Art Activity

3. Have each student use butcher paper to create a map of his or her life. This map should include a starting point and a destination, as well as most of the items listed on the worksheet. For example, a student's map might include the island of loneliness, the third grade ocean, the mountains of arguing with parents, the cool streams of friendships, the musical national forest and the badlands of divorce.

   Encourage the use of creative land forms, colors, and other features.

   Once students have finished their maps, they should use a wide black marker to clearly delineate (using a dashed or dotted line) the route they have taken or navigated so far.

✍️ Writing Activity

4. Have students write a narrative description of their life journeys as depicted on the maps. These should be metaphorical in nature saying things like "sailing across the family sea, sometimes fearing shipwreck and other times enjoying the cool salt air," rather than "dealing with the good and bad parts of my family."

Evaluation

- Students' use of metaphors to describe life's experiences
- Creativity of map and geographical/experiential features included in it
- Descriptive written account of student's journey

Extensions

Obstacles - Ask students to write about the mountains they have climbed or oceans they have crossed.

Future Trip - Have students plan a trip to a future destination.

Mapping Life's Journey

Tell how the following geographical items might represent experiences in your life. For example, an ocean may represent a difficult crossing or troubled part of your life, such as losing a friend. A rest stop may be a break from the typical experience and could be something such as a family reunion or gathering.

Map items   **What they represent in my life**

mountains   _____

highways   _____

smaller, less traveled roads   _____

rivers   _____

rural areas or farmland   _____

capitol city   _____

island   _____

ocean   _____

beach   _____

forest   _____

canyons   _____

national parks   _____

rest stops   _____

YARD SALE SOLUTION

Overview

Students will focus on making self-improvements by identifying outgrown coping mechanisms and negative behaviors that clutter up their lives and making "for sale" signs for these behaviors or attitudes.

Objectives

- The student will demonstrate self-evaluation in terms of identifying negative attitudes, habits, or behaviors.
- The student will identify sources of stress in his or her life and pose possible solutions.

Materials Needed

✓ copies of page 57
✓ art supplies for creation of signs
✓ poster board or cardboard

Procedure

❝ Discussion

1. Ask students if they have been to or had a yard sale or garage sale. Ask them why people have these sales and elicit some of these responses:

- to get rid of clutter
- to sell things they have outgrown or no longer need
- to make room for new things

Ask students how easy they think it is to put a price on things they have enjoyed, even though they may not use them any more.

Discuss preparation for the yard sale. Make sure you elicit some of these responses from students:
- you have to clean up the clutter
- you have to decide what to sell and what to keep
- you have to advertise and price the items you are selling

Finally, ask students to picture their lives as a big house they are going to clean out for a yard sale. Have them think about what behaviors they no longer need or would be better off without. Discuss some negative behaviors, thoughts, social patterns, or coping mechanisms that cause trouble for people. Examples might include gossiping, being careless, fighting, having a short temper, having poor study habits, or speaking without thinking. These behaviors are things that prevent us from being the best we can be or from relating well to other people. Talk about how hard it is to change these behaviors.

2. Distribute copies of page 57. Have students analyze their past behavior or actions and decide what they would most want to get rid of. Have them write these behaviors on the yard sale signs on the handout. Ask students how easy it will be to give up these behaviors or replace them with more positive behaviors. Have them set the price accordingly. Explain that when they get rid of these bad habits, they will have more room in their lives for positive thoughts and actions.

✍ Writing Activity

3. Have students select one of the issues or behaviors written on a yard sale sign and write a paragraph telling more about it. The writing should follow this format:

- Give a real-life example
- Tell why it is best to get rid of it
- Tell how they plan to get rid of this behavior, habit or attitude and what new behavior will take its place

✂ Art Activity

4. Have students create a large poster or sign to sell the behavior they wrote about in the writing activity. Encourage students to be creative by adding decorations to the posters or by enhancing them with pop-outs or three-dimensional features.

Evaluation

- Identification of objectives for self improvement
- Creativity of poster to advertise the selected item
- Well-organized paragraph about one behavior

Extensions

Not for Sale - Ask students to write about some things that they would never sell for any amount of money.

Want Ad - Discuss the fact that one person's trash is another person's treasure. Have students write newspaper ads for something they wish to sell. Then have them respond to these ads from the point of view of someone else who would like to purchase the objects.

A World-wide Application - Have students identify behaviors that mankind as a whole would be better off without. These might be behaviors like greed, intolerance, or prejudice. Divide the class into small groups and ask each group to choose a behavior. Then have them orally give examples of this behavior or act out a short skit that demonstrates the behavior. They should then explain why the world would be better without this behavior or attitude.

YARD SALE ITEMS

Fill in the yard sale signs below with items from your life that you would like to "clean out." Each sign represents something in your life (a behavior, attitude or emotion) that you would like to dispose of. After all signs are filled in, place a price on each one.

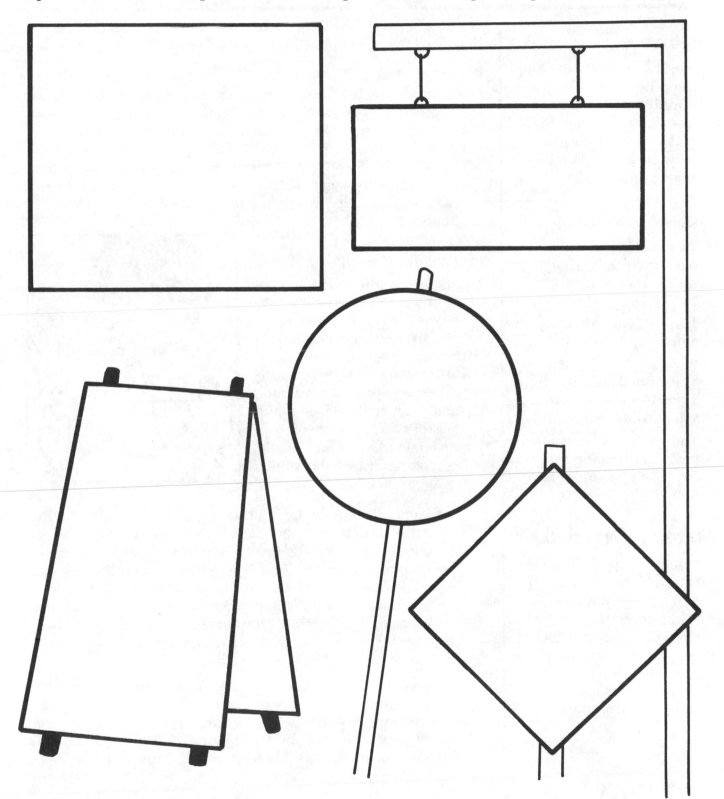

Let the Sun Shine In

Overview

Using the sun as a symbol of happiness and self-fulfillment, students will write about the positive aspects of their lives and create a complementary art project.

Objectives

- The student will write a poem that tells what makes him or her happy.
- The student will analyze what makes him or her happy.
- The student will develop a positive awareness of self and life factors.
- The student will create a piece of art using the sun as a symbol for happiness.

Materials Needed

- ✓ copies of pages 60 - 63
- ✓ watercolors, crayons, and colored pencils
- ✓ construction paper
- ✓ black felt tipped pens
- ✓ sponges cut into small pieces (optional)
- ✓ sketchbook paper or white drawing paper

Procedure

66 Discussion

1. Ask the students to brainstorm positive influences found in our country today. List each of these on the rays of a sun that you have drawn on the chalkboard or on a large sheet of butcher paper. Initiate a class discussion about what makes people happy and encourage students to share their happiest memories. Discuss the symbolism of the sun as a metaphor for happiness. Examples: it gives light and warmth or is bright and cheerful in color.

Writing Activity

2. Ask each student to fill out the questionnaire entitled "What Makes Me Shine?" (pages 60 - 61). These questionnaires should serve as a means for students to reflect on the positive aspects of their lives but should not be displayed in the classroom. They may be very personal in nature and should be kept in individual portfolios or journals.

Have students refer to the information on their questionnaires to help them write the poem "The Sun Shines for Me (page 62). Pass out the sample poem (page 63) and go over it before students begin their own writing. The guidelines for the poem are clearly defined on the student worksheet, but it is important to mention that all responses should be descriptive in nature, not simply listed. For example: *The sun* shines for me when I see tall, majestic mountains," NOT *"The sun shines for me when I see mountains."*

When finished, the poems should be neatly written or typed and superimposed on top of the sun art project explained below. Students may choose to copy the words in the shape of the sun, rather than in straight parallel lines. They should eliminate all words in parentheses that were used on the worksheet.

✂ Art Activity

3. Have each student design a creative sun that represents happiness for him or her. They should begin this activity by sketching many different sun designs, using designs in which the rays are shown in a variety of unusual ways.

Students should experiment with a variety of materials and colors to create suns that are both unique and attractive. At least three colors should be used in the artwork. Students should not be discouraged from using unusual color schemes for their suns.

Some examples of suns might be:

a. A watercolor design covering the entire page in an abstract form
b. Cut or torn pieces of paper, such as magazine pages or construction paper, that create mosaic suns
c. Sponge painted sun designs
d. Realistic suns colored attractively using watercolors, crayons, markers, or colored pencils.

Evaluation

- Vividness of descriptions used in the poem
- Art to complement and enhance the poem

Extensions

Essay - Assign an essay entitled "My Sunshine," in which the students write about the wonderful things happening in their lives at the present time. The essay should be 500 words in length and of a creative nature.

Definition - Ask students to define the word "happiness" in a descriptive paragraph.

Short Story - Assign a short story based on a pleasant memory from each student's past. Students may wish to fictionalize their accounting of the story.

What Makes Me Shine?

Fill out this questionnaire as honestly as you can. Answer a minimum of 12 of the 16 questions. Be very thorough and think in positive terms.

1. The three best things going on in my life at the present time are _____

_____

_____

2. The best thing about my family is _____

_____

3. I am proud of my ability to _____

_____

4. The hardest thing I ever had to do was,_____
   but I am proud of myself for accomplishing it.

5. The two happiest memories of my life thus far are _____

_____

_____

6. The type of music that makes me the happiest is _____

7. The two people who have the ability to make me laugh are _____

_____

8. Some things I laugh about are _____

_____

9. The things I like best about myself are_____

_____

10. If I could be remembered for one thing in my life it would be _____
_____

11. I am a good friend because _____
_____

12. The most positive word or phrase that best describes me is _____
_____

13. My favorite time of day is _____, because _____
_____

14. Tastes that bring back happy memories are _____
_____

15. The smells I love to remember are _____
_____

16. Choose the natural environment you enjoy the most and explain why.

mountains	desert	the country
ocean	the forest	other

_____

_____

_____

The Sun Shines For Me

Fill in each of the elements of the poem using the following guidelines. Each prompt should have at least two responses. Each response should be short, vivid, and descriptive.

The Sun Shines for Me

When I see *(visual memories)* _____

_____

When I hear *(sounds that have made you happy)* _____

_____

When I smell or taste *(pleasant memories of smells or tastes)* _____

_____

When I am able to *(accomplishments or ability to do something)* _____

_____

When I am with *(family, friends, pets)* _____

_____

When I go to *(places that make you happy)* _____

_____

The sun shines for me. *(End your poem with these words.)*

The Sun Shines for Me
Sample Poem

The sun shines for me . . .

When I see tall, majestic mountains in the morning sun and the accepting faces of those I love,

When I hear the booming base from my favorite song pulsing from the radio speaker and the sound of the wind whispering softly through the trees,

When I smell the delicious aroma of food at the fair and the fresh powdery scent of a newborn baby,

When I taste a delicious bite of warm chocolate pie fresh from the oven, or a sweet, juicy watermelon on a hot summer day,

When I am able to immerse myself in a compelling novel, accomplish small tasks that I've managed to put off for days, and to make good grades in my class work,

When I am with my family, my very best friends Teneshia and Matthew, or my adorable pet poodle "Pookie,"

When I go to a Friday night football game on a crisp fall evening, or a warm, sunny beach in the middle of summer,

The sun shines for me.

A Measure of Virtue

Overview

Students will explore virtues and positive personal qualities such as courage, tolerance, and kindness through discussion, writing, and graphing.

Objective

- The student will give examples of virtues and positive character traits.
- The student will analyze different social situations in terms of the chosen virtues.
- The student will write a paragraph or poem on a positive personality trait.
- The student will create a graph to depict a virtue.

Materials Needed

- ✓ butcher paper and markers
- ✓ copies of page 66
- ✓ construction paper, scissors, glue
- ✓ crayons or markers

Procedure

66 Discussion

1. Facilitate a discussion about courage. Differentiate between courage and foolhardiness. Help students understand that courage means doing the right thing, even when it is difficult or risky, whereas foolhardiness merely means you'll try anything. Discuss the different motivations behind courageous and foolhardy acts.

Ask the class to generate a list of situations that require courage. Record their responses on the board or butcher paper. These might include, but not be limited to:
- admitting to a mistake
- volunteering an answer that might not be right
- meeting new people or being in unfamiliar situations
- being friends with an unpopular person
- sticking up for your beliefs
- being different
- defying peer pressure
- trying something new
- following rules when no one else is doing so

Graphing

2. Ask students to individually rate each of the actions you have listed in step one in terms of the amount of courage needed, using a scale of 1 to 5 (1 being no courage required, 5 being all the courage you have in you).

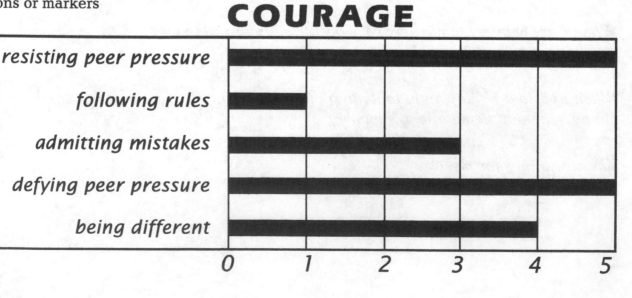

COURAGE

	0	1	2	3	4	5
resisting peer pressure						
following rules						
admitting mistakes						
defying peer pressure						
being different						

Distribute copies of page 66. Have students use their individual ratings to make a bar graph on the handout. This graph should depict the amount of courage they feel is required in nine of the situations they rated.

When students have completed this activity, ask them to assemble in groups of 3-4 and compare their graphs. Lead them into discovering that the level of courage required in different situations is different for all people. Help students recognize the value of these differences.

66 Discussion

3. Ask students what other virtues or positive character traits are needed in their daily interactions with others. Record student responses and try to elicit the following:

- kindness
- patience
- tolerance
- compassion
- integrity
- mercy

Discuss each of these virtues. Then have each student select one virtue to explore further.

⁓ Graphing / Art Activity

4. Now have students get into groups of 2 to 4 and generate (on scratch paper) a list of situations in which they would need their selected virtue, rate them as in the previous exercise, and create a graph using posterboard or butcher paper and grab bag supplies that shows the level of that trait needed in the situations they listed. They can use pictures or three-dimensional objects to represent the numbers on their graphs.

✍ Writing Activity

5. Ask students to write descriptive paragraphs or poem about their selected virtues, defining the importance of the trait, giving examples of when it is demonstrated and when it is missing from social situations.

Students can then mount their individual descriptive paragraphs or poems with their group graphs. They should add pictures and decorations to make the final project more attractive and illustrative.

Evaluation

- Creativity in constructing the graph depicting the selected virtue
- Creativity and depth of thought of poem or paragraph describing the selected virtue
- Evidence of evaluative thinking regarding the selected virtue and the situations in which it is required

Extensions

Writing - Have students write true stories about someone who has demonstrated courage.

Research - Have students research famous people to find people who have demonstrated various virtues – compassion, courage, mercy, forgiveness, selflessness, honesty, dependability, faithfulness, giving.

How Much Courage?

Select nine situations that require courage and write these in the boxes. Use your individual ratings to shade in the graph depicting the amount of courage you feel is required in each of these situations.

Situations   **How Much Courage is Required**

1. Admitting to a mistake	1	2	3	4	5
2.	1	2	3	4	5
3.	1	2	3	4	5
4.	1	2	3	4	5
5.	1	2	3	4	5
6.	1	2	3	4	5
7.	1	2	3	4	5
8.	1	2	3	4	5
9.	1	2	3	4	5

My Gift to the World

Overview

Students will create gifts that represent kind actions, feelings, or acceptance they have received or would like to give to others.

Objectives

- The student will recognize the value of giving.
- The student will write four short paragraphs on the subject of gifts.
- The student will make a creative art project on which to display the written work.

Materials Needed

- ✓ copies of page 69
- ✓ unlined white paper
- ✓ watercolors, markers, crayons, and colored pencils
- ✓ grab bag of materials that includes shiny papers, ribbons of different colors and sizes, wallpaper samples, and unlined index cards
- ✓ small sponges of varying sizes

Procedure

❝ Discussion

1. Discuss the concept of gift-giving and occasions when people give gifts. Ask students to generate a list of gifts that are not concrete, such as time, services rendered, or an act of kindness. It is important to emphasize that it's the thought and the kindness extended that really matters.

Brainstorm the possible meanings of the term "random acts of kindness" and list examples of these deeds. Help students to understand that a random act of kindness doesn't always bring glory or recognition to the person doing the act. The reward, if any, is often just a smile, a thank-you, or the self-satisfaction that comes from knowing that you did a good thing.

✍ Writing Activity

2. Distribute copies of page 69. Ask students to write a paragraph on each of the four topics. Have students incorporate the writing activities with their (or your) choice of the art activities that follow.

✂ Art Activity

3. Select one of the following ways to design presents:

   a. Use shiny wrapping paper, ribbon and glitter from the class grab bag to create a collage of presents. Write each of the four written responses on gift tags made from unlined index cards. Attach the gift tags with ribbon to the four presents.

   b. Use watercolors with sponges to design an attractive page of four presents. Write the four different paragraphs in black pen, one on each of the four packages.

   c. Wrap one box with gift wrap (easy gift-wrap can be made by stamping designs on brown craft paper). Put each of the writer's responses on index cards and attach all four with ribbon as if they were gift tags.

   d. Design a page with one large present and write the paragraphs within the borders of the gift.

Evaluation

- Quality of ideas incorporated into the writing assignment
- Creativity of gift design

Extensions

Research - Have students research gift-giving traditions in other cultures.

Give to Others - Have students make a list of ways that they can help people who are less fortunate or make a positive contribution to their community. Then have them select one idea and implement it.

Personal Story - Have students write essays in which they describes times when they helped someone or had an impact on someone's life.

Think carefully about the meaning of the word "gift." Write a paragraph to complete each of the following starters.

My gift to the world _____

_____

_____

_____

The best gift I ever received _____

_____

_____

_____

The best random act of kindness directed toward me _____

_____

_____

_____

The best random act of kindness I have done for someone else _____

_____

_____

_____

Places in the Heart

Overview

Students will select several special places where they have lived or visited and use these places as a basis for a writing and a drawing project.

Objectives

- The student will identify positive feelings about past memories.
- The student will write about a special place.
- The student will make a mural to represent several of his or her special places.

Materials Needed

✓ scratch paper and drawing paper
✓ copies of page 72
✓ markers, watercolors, or colored pencils
✓ glue and scissors

Procedure

✍ Writing Activity

1. Distribute copies of page 72. Ask students to list places that have special memories for them.

Have students select one special place and write a descriptive paragraph about it. This paragraph should present a visual picture of the place, include descriptions that appeal to all the senses, and explain why the place is so special to them.

✂ Art Activity

2. Ask students to design a mural that consists of at least eight places in a row, complete with landscaping and natural features. These houses, buildings and natural features should represent a time line of students' past memories. The choice of places to put in the mural could be outdoor places (parks, mountains, etc.) as well as buildings (homes, schools, stores, libraries, museums). Each item in the drawing should be touching the one next to it. If students wish, they may use photographs or magazine pictures for the mural. The places depicted are symbolic of the actual places, so it is not necessary to make them look like the real thing.

After the mural has been colored or painted, have students carefully write the names of the places on the buildings or geographical features. These names can be written on tiny little signs and actual street numbers can be used.

Evaluation

- Vividness of the descriptive paragraph
- Representation of important places in student's life on mural

Extension

Postcard - Have students create postcards for their special places. On the back they can write a message telling why they are fond of this place.

Places in the Heart

List all of the places from your past that have special memories for you. Try to generate a list of at least 20 places.

1. _____
2. _____
3. _____
4. _____
5. _____
6. _____
7. _____
8. _____
9. _____
10. _____

11. _____
12. _____
13. _____
14. _____
15. _____
16. _____
17. _____
18. _____
19. _____
20. _____

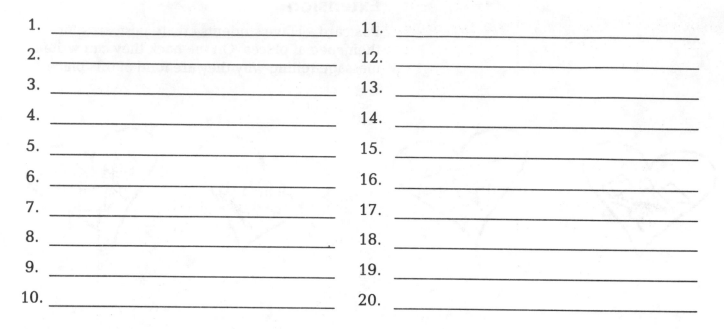

Select your most special place and write a descriptive paragraph about it.

_____

_____

_____

_____

_____

Continue of the back of this paper if you need more room.

A Recipe for Friendship

Overview

Students use the recipe format to identify the ingredients of a positive relationship.

Objectives

- The student will identify the character traits of a friend.
- The student will select the most important personal qualities and behaviors and use them to write a recipe for friendship.

Materials

✓ pen or pencils and paper
✓ recipe cards
✓ cookbooks

Procedure

66 Discussion

1. Discuss friendship using the following questions.
   - What do you like about having a friend?
   - What are some things that your friends do that you like?
   - On what do you think friendship is based?
   - What are the qualities that you look for in a friend?
   - What kind of character traits do good friends have?

As a group, generate a list of ingredients for a friendship.

✍ Writing Activity

2. Distribute cookbooks and ask students to examine the recipe format. Note the list of ingredients, the measurements and proportions, the instructions for blending and mixing, the cooking temperature, and the serving instructions.

Pass out page 75 and review the sample recipe.

Have students utilize this format to create a friendship recipe using some of the items from the generated list of ingredients. Each person's recipe should reflect what he or she thinks is important in a friendship, and the proportions should indicate the relative importance of the ingredients.

Use the following questions to discuss the final products.
- Will you slowly blend the first ingredients before adding the rest or will you stir them all together briskly? Why?
- Will you have more of some ingredients than others? Why?
- Will you cook your recipe at a high temperature in the oven or simmer it on the stove top? Why?

✄ Art Activity

3. Have students write their recipes on recipe cards and decorate the cards with images of things they are interested in. Post these on the bulletin board.

Evaluation

- Creativity of the recipe cards
- Inclusion of positive friendship qualities in the recipes

Extensions

Drama - Give students an opportunity to dramatize cooks who are showing others how to cook their special recipes. Have them present their recipes in an animated fashion as cooks on television do. As they add each ingredient they should explain why they are using this ingredient.

Other Attributes - Have students create recipes for a good student, a good teacher, a good parent, or a good child.

From the Kitchen of Jorge Rodriguez

For an enjoyable and healthy friendship, blend together :

    1 cup interest in baseball
    3/4 cup ability to laugh
    a dash of craziness

Simmer over low heat.
When sufficiently warm, add:

    3 tablespoons of loyalty
    4 teaspoons of trust

Top with a sprinkling of time spent together in the past mixed with plans for the future. Best when nutured on a daily basis.

From the Kitchen of Kimberly Brown

For an enjoyable and healthy friendship, blend together :

    1 cup shared interests
    3/4 cup time spent together
    a dash of fun

Simmer over low heat.
When sufficiently warm, add:

    3 tablespoons of trust
    4 teaspoons of understanding

Top with a sprinkling of unconditional love.
Best when served warm. Appeals to all tastes.

A Recipe for Friendship

Sample

From the Kitchen of __Sample__

For an enjoyable and healthy friendship, blend together :

> *1 cup shared interests*
> *3/4 cup time spent together*
> *a dash of fun*

Simmer over low heat.
When sufficiently warm, add:

> *3 tablespoons of trust*
> *4 teaspoons of understanding*

Top with a sprinkling of unconditional love.
Best when served warm. Appeals to all tastes.

PICK - A - STORY

Overview

Students will combine a random selection of story elements into a short story that allows them to explore emotions and relationships.

Objectives

- The student will analyze the social and emotional needs of others.
- The student will demonstrate creative writing skills.

Materials Needed

✓ writing paper
✓ pens or pencils
✓ watercolors, markers, crayons, or colored pencils
✓ numerals 0-9 written on small pieces of paper
✓ container to put above items in for drawing
✓ copies of page 77

Procedure

✍ Writing Activity

1. Have students select four numbers in one of two ways:
   - randomly draw four numbers from 0-9
   - Use the last 4 digits of a phone number or social security number

Record these numbers for future reference.

Distribute copies of page 77. Discuss the categories mentioned in each column. Tell students that they will be composing a story based on the numbers they selected. Their first number will indicate the numbered item they are to choose from the first column, the second number should correspond with a numbered item in the second column, and so on. Have students write a short story based on their particular random combination of numbers. For example, if their numbers were 1-6-9-4, their story would be about a child/pet relationship, guilt, a small town, and extremely hot and humid weather. Each student should put him or herself in the story in order to process the emotion in a more personal and meaningful way.

✂ Art Activity

2. When students have finished writing their stories, have them create unique cover designs and incorporate three illustrations into the bodies of their stories. These stories can be made into hardcover books, or all of them can be compiled into a class book.

Evaluation

- Development of a relationship and interaction between characters
- Portrayal of an emotion
- Use of the four elements of the story
- Creativity of the story

Extension

Improv Stories - Have students create and act out stories based on unrelated topics or categories selected randomly.

PICK-A-STORY

Select four random digits between 0 and 9. Circle the number in the first column that corresponds with your first number. Circle the number in the second column that corresponds to your second number, and so on. Combine the circled items from each of the categories to create a creative short story involving the relationship and emotions of the assigned characters.

Relationship	Emotion	Setting	Weather
0. child / pet	0. love	0. seashore	0. thunderstorm
1. parent / child	1. hope	1. mountains	1. snow
2. brother / sister	2. anger	2. forest	2. ice
3. three friends	3. fear	3. big city	3. fog
4. divorced parents	4. loneliness	4. ranch or farm	4. extremely hot and humid
5. boyfriend/girlfriend	5. sadness	5. island	5. crisp and cold
6. total strangers	6. guilt	6. rainforest	6. gentle rain
7. grandparent / grandchild	7. embarrassment	7. foreign country	7. cloudy or overcast
8. three classmates who are not friends	8. despair	8. desert	8. balmy or spring-like
9. stepparent / stepchild	9. joy	9. small town	9. natural disaster

Appendix 1
Personality Traits

accepting	flexible	outgoing
active	friendly	passive
ambitious	fun-loving	patient
amicable	generous	playful
assertive	gentle	polite
bashful	good friend	problem solver
boastful	good listener	resilient
brave	good natured	resourceful
caring	gregarious	sensitive
cheerful	grouchy	serious
compassionate	hard-working	shy
conceited	helpful	sincere
considerate	honest	skeptical
cooperative	honorable	slow to anger
courageous	happy	sociable
creative	kind	stingy
curious	neat	stubborn
dependable	loyal	thoughtful
determined	mischievous	timid
diplomatic	modest	tolerant
disobedient	moody	trustworthy
easy-going	open to new experiences	truthful
fair	optimistic	understanding
fearful	organized	up-tight

Appendix 2
Feelings

aggravated

angry

annoyed

anxious

at ease

blissful

blue

bored

calm

cautious

cheerful

concerned

confused

contented

delighted

desperate

disgusted

displeased

distressed

down-in-the-dumps

distressed

embarrassed

excited

fearful

frustrated

gratified

guilty

happy

helpless

hopeful

hurt

ill at ease

irritated

jealous

joyful

mad

melancholy

merry

miserable

nervous

offended

overjoyed

overwhelmed

pleased

proud

puzzled

regretful

relaxed

relieved

resentful

sad

shocked

sorrowful

surprised

tranquil

uncomfortable

unconcerned

uneasy

unhappy

victimized

weary

worried

Appendix 3
Recipes

Paper Mâché Paste

Recipe 1 (easiest):
Go to the hardware store and purchase a package of wallpaper paste (in powder form, not pre-mixed). Mix the paste with water as directed.

Recipe 2
2 parts water
1 part white glue (not the water-soluble school glue)

Recipe 3
1 cup flour
2 teaspoons white glue
2 cups boiling water

Make a creamy paste with the flour and a little cold water, then add the boiling water and the glue. Mix well.

Start with some kind of base (cardboard, wood, balloon). Tear newspapers, butcher paper, or plain white paper into strips so they are no more than an inch wide. Dip the strips into the paste. Squeeze excess paste from the strips. Apply to the base shape and smooth. Repeat until entire surface is completely covered. Let this layer dry and apply at least one more layer to the surface. When completely dry, paper mâché surface may be painted or sealed.

Paper Mâché Clay

Tear old newspapers into one-inch squares and soak them overnight in a bucket of water. Pour off most of the liquid and use an electric mixer to beat the newspaper bits to a pulp. Squeeze out the excess water. Add wheat paste (from wallpaper store) and beat until you have a thick, smooth mixture. Add a few drops of wintergreen oil if desired to help preserve the compound. When molded into pottery, jewelry, or small sculpture, the clay will take 3 to 5 days to dry. It can then be sanded, painted, and sealed.